# Daring to Dream
## Sherpa women climbing K2

By Frances Klatzel as told by Dawa Yangzum Sherpa, Maya Sherpa and Pasang Lhamu Sherpa Akita

Illustrations by Alina Chhantel

Published by Mera Publications Pvt. Ltd.
2020

Daring to Dream
Sherpa women climbing K2

Published by Mera Publications Pvt. Ltd., March 2020
ISBN No. 978-9937-0-7178-9

First edition: March 2020

Mera Publications Pvt. Ltd.
PO Box 21415, Kathmandu, Nepal
Phone: 977 1 4650723
Email: merapublications@gmail.com

Design and Printing: Digiscan Pre-press Pvt. Ltd., Kathmandu. Phone: 4428572
Email: dgscan.mail@gmail.com

MAP OF NEPAL AND PAKISTAN

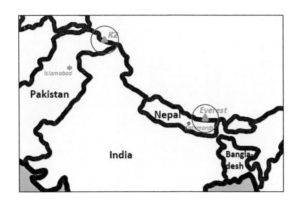

*"As human beings we should all have a dream. Our dream motivates us to go further in our life.*

*"Thanks to support from my husband and my family I am what I am today. Young people with big dreams need family support. Each of us should follow our dreams. It takes hard work and dedication. Nothing comes easily, but afterwards the success is so precious."*

*Maya Sherpa*

*The Bottleneck traverse*

# FOREWORDS

This story of three, strong Nepali women will inspire anyone to go for their dream. In this candidly depicted journey to K2 – the 'savage' mountain – Dawa Yangzum Sherpa, Maya Sherpa and Pasang Lhamu Sherpa Akita open up about not only the physical challenge of climbing itself, but the added limitations placed upon them as women. They were told that their dreams were unachievable, and that they should instead settle for the stereotypical gendered role of taking care of their family. The readers will learn that it was their hard work and teamwork that eventually helped them succeed.

**Pasang Yangjee Sherpa PhD**
Anthropologist

I was one of the climbers sharing the mountain with Pasang, Maya, and Dawa on this K2 climb. They are great role models for girls in Nepal and globally, and show that you too can live your life with passion if you follow your dreams. I always say that success on the mountain is a waste of time if it is not used to motivate others. How can you not learn and grow by the challenges of climbing a mountain? Life is all about challenges, it's having the courage to fall down and the strength to get back up; courage changes everything. It's daring to dream. Be BOLD in your DREAMS! Live your life. Don't leave your dreams on your pillow.

**Al Hancock**
Key Note Speaker and Alpinist

Over the past couple of decades, we have had the extraordinary pleasure of befriending some of the diverse people that are the rich fabric of Nepal's culture. It has been exciting to see the growing leadership role of mountain people and Nepali climbers. We feel so very honored to know Dawa Yangzum Sherpa, Pasang Lhamu Sherpa Akita, and Maya Sherpa, and to witness their perseverance. From humble beginnings of hardship to heroines who are giving back to their country of Nepal in a variety of ways, these young women are an inspiration to all.

**Jenni Lowe-Anker and Conrad Anker**
Founders, Khumbu Climbing Centre

*In the Bottleneck*

# INTRODUCTION

*The Bottleneck traverse*

**Dawa:** *"I took a step forward, my crampons gripping the smooth ice sloping down over the cliffs.*

*"Here we stood on this narrow ledge on K2. Now I understood why people call it the 'savage' mountain. I breathed deep. I was so scared. A wall of glacier ice hung above us and nothing but ice-covered cliffs falling thousands of feet below. We were so close to, but so far from the summit.*

*"Step by step, each of us inched across the steep ice of the 'Bottleneck,' the most dangerous part of the climb. If the ice above broke, it could either sweep us off the cliff or cut the rope so we could not descend the mountain.*

*"Even though I had lived in a world of ice and snow since I was a girl, I had never been in such a dangerous place."*

# CHAPTER 1:
# OUR INDIVIDUAL STORIES

*Eleven year old Dawa carrying water over ice and snow.*

# DAWA
## Difficulty and Courage

I was born in Rolwaling, a small valley high in the Himalaya to the west of the Mount Everest region. My family had yaks and land so my father was busy as a farmer. He sometimes worked as a trekking guide, but mostly he stayed in Rolwaling.

When I was six years old, my uncle and aunt took me to Kathmandu for an education. I went to school in the city until I was ten. One day on the street in Kathmandu, I saw a rally with Sherpa women celebrating their Everest expedition in 2000. Seeing them and hearing about the first Nepali woman to climb Everest made me start thinking about what I wanted to do in my life.

Eventually, my aunt and uncle got divorced so I had to return to the village and do all the chores in my family. We did not have any electricity or running water to our house.

In spring and summer, going to the spring to bring water took just ten minutes, but in winter, going and coming took an hour with the huge container full of water wiggling on my back.

I was afraid to take a step. Ice covered the rocky trail. Around the ice, the snow was waist high. With each step, I could slip and fall, losing drops of the precious water. I was just eleven years old.

You could say that my chores were the start of my preparation for the hardships of climbing difficult mountains.

Rolwaling had an old school, but the teachers came from the lowland, warmer parts of Nepal. There were no heaters in the school, so the teachers and the children did not come during the cold winters. I dropped out of school after class four.

My mother died when I was fifteen, so my older brothers and I had to take care of our two younger brothers. We lived our lives day by day.

As a child I always heard about the "kangri-pa" – the men who went to work on the snow peaks to make a living for their families. They would come back to the village in the summer monsoon with fancy clothes in blue plastic drums. I was fascinated to see them.

*Dawa carrying a trekking load over the pass.*

We were all the Sherpa ethnic group in the Himalaya, but these men worked as 'sherpa' guides and climbers on the expeditions to climb high peaks.

Foreign trekkers would occasionally hike up to our valley to go over Tashi Lapcha Pass into the Everest area. When I was thirteen, a friend and I ran away with one of these trekking groups that hired us as extra porters. This was my first time working.

To cross the pass into Khumbu, we had to walk on rocks and the glacier ice while stones fell from the cliffs above. We carried 30 kg loads for six days across this difficult pass. Once we got to Thame village in Khumbu, I was eager to go down to Kathmandu to see what I could do to follow my dreams.

My friend went back to Rolwaling with another trekking group, but I walked down the Khumbu

14

valley to Lukla, then took my first airplane flight out to Kathmandu. I stayed with my brothers while I took classes to be a trekking guide. Slowly, I started working as a trekking guide, while still just a teenager.

At seventeen in 2008, I was staying in my village for a month. Two American climbers, Joe and David, came to climb the mountain just above our houses. I would chitchat with them about climbing. I was the only girl in my village who could speak English, which I had learned from my time in Kathmandu and my trekking work.

Joe and David called me when they came back to climb in Rolwaling. I let them stay in my home free of cost. Getting all the gear for climbing is expensive, but Joe was sponsored

*Joe and David in Dawa's home.*

15

by Sherpa Adventure Gear, so he gave me gear made by this company. Joe and David were big supporters of my climbing career as they first showed me the path.

I wanted to be a trekking guide, but never imagined that I could become a climber until I heard about a one-month climbing course with Nepal Mountaineering Association. I paid for the course with the money I had earned from trekking work.

There were only five girls among the 42 people in the training and I was the youngest person in the course, just 18 at that time. I quickly learned all the techniques. I felt strong, so I thought I could keep doing this. After the training, I earned more money working on trips to climb peaks.

When I was first starting as a climber, I heard about other women climbers, Pasang and Maya. Eventually, Pasang and I climbed Ama Dablam together. Since then, Pasang and I have worked together many times as guides on smaller peaks and I came to know Maya as well. She is twelve years older than me and has a lot of climbing experience. I think that although Pasang and I are stronger than Maya physically, she is mentally stronger than either of us. I really like this quality about her.

We are all comfortable with each other in the mountains so we decided to climb a big mountain together. Pasang and Maya had been planning to climb K2 since 2008, even before I started climbing. It took years for the whole idea to finally come together, while Maya had a baby and Pasang was busy with other work.

# PASANG
## Dreams and Plans

I was born in Khumjung, a small village near Everest, but my mother moved to Lukla when I was little. To make money to raise my sister and I, my mother ran a small teashop here at the airport for the Everest region in Lukla.

As a kid, I would roam around Lukla and climb trees. I washed cups to help my mother at her teashop while I watched the tourists coming to climb our mountains.

Every morning in the spring and fall, groups of trekkers and mountaineers would walk past me as I squatted at the door of the teashop washing glasses with my hands wet, even in the freezing weather.

I always heard that these foreigners were going up the valley to climb the mountains. It was especially exciting when they were going to climb Everest. I wanted so badly to be like these foreigners, to keep walking up the trail to climb the mountains.

I have the same name as the first Nepali woman to climb Mt. Everest, Pasang Lhamu Sherpa.

Unfortunately, she died on the way down from the summit so I never met her. She was famous.

When I told people my name, they would say you have to climb Mount Everest. That encouraged me to climb mountains. Then it became my aim and dream.

I went to school a 15-minute walk from my home in the big village below Lukla. On the way to school, I would walk with the tourists and talk to them about their trek or climb.

My mother died when I was in grade 10. Instead of my dream, I had to take care of my sister and myself. It was difficult. All the responsibilities came down on me at once. I stopped dreaming like other young people because I worried about my sister's and my future.

The board exams were coming, and I did not know what to do without my mother. I almost dropped out from school, but all my friends, teachers, and relatives convinced me to stay in school and complete my School Leaving Certificate.

*Pasang helping to wash dishes
in her mother's teashop.*

*Pasang talking to trekkers on her way to school.*

I rented our teashop to a relative and stayed with them. They ran the business making tea and momos, while my sister and I went to school.

After my examinations, I went to live with my cousin and her husband in their rented apartment in Kathmandu. I stayed with them for two years until I completed grade 12.

In the long school vacations, I went back to the mountains to help my aunt run her lodge and restaurant in Phortse, since I no longer had any family in Lukla. While I was in Phortse cooking

19

for my aunt, I met some Spanish trekkers. They asked if I liked to cook. I answered "No, I want to climb."

They were planning to organize a trek for women and asked if I was interested to go with them. After six months, they wrote to ask if I wanted to learn Spanish, because they wanted to hire me as a trekking guide in Khumbu.

This was an exciting opportunity. They sent me money to pay for language classes and expenses. By taking the language classes at the less expensive government university in Kathmandu, I was able to save enough money to live and take more climbing courses.

I attended training with Khumbu Climbing Centre and Nepal Mountaineering Association. I had seen women going climbing on Everest, but no woman guiding on mountains. I decided that I wanted to become a mountaineering instructor because as a teacher, people respect you. Mountaineering is a male-dominated profession so many parents may not feel secure to send their daughters to mountaineering training. I thought if there is at least one-woman instructor, other women who followed me might feel more comfortable.

Still, many people discouraged me. "It is men's work, just stay at home," they said. I was in a dilemma, whether it was a good thing to do or not, but I decided to make it my profession. I always wanted to be on a mountain, and I wanted to encourage other women.

Nobody knows what difficulties we face as women. We fear what society will say. People might talk behind our backs seeing us working with men. With one struggle after another, we become stronger as our confidence develops.

Every year the Nepal Mountaineering Association has exams to select three candidates to go to France for further training and a diploma course on mountaineering. I worked hard and was selected. After the training, I came back and started working as an instructor. People started respecting me. The teasing stopped. Being an instructor offered me protection.

To commemorate 50 years of diplomatic relations between Nepal and Japan, the Nepal Mountaineering Association (NMA) and the Japan Workers Alpine Federation (JWAF) jointly organized a mountaineering expedition in autumn 2006 to Nangpai Gosum. One member from each participating climbing association was to join the expedition and I was chosen to represent Nepal's Mountain Guide Association. I would have the chance to climb this unclimbed peak to the south-west of Cho Oyu Himal.

Unfortunately, the leader of the Japanese expedition team refused at first to include me in that expedition saying it was too tough and technical. I was embarrassed because that was the first opportunity for me to do a 7000 m mountain and I did not want to lose that opportunity.

Finally, the president of the Nepal Mountaineering Association convinced the Japanese leader saying that I would just go on the expedition but stay at base camp and that NMA would cover all my expenses.

I worked very hard in that expedition to show my capabilities - cooking food every day, carrying a two-meter tall bag with climbing equipment. I gave my best effort and finally the Japanese were convinced of my skills so I got the chance to climb Nangpai Gosum, a very hard unclimbed mountain.

*Pasang with back problems at Everest Basecamp.*

21

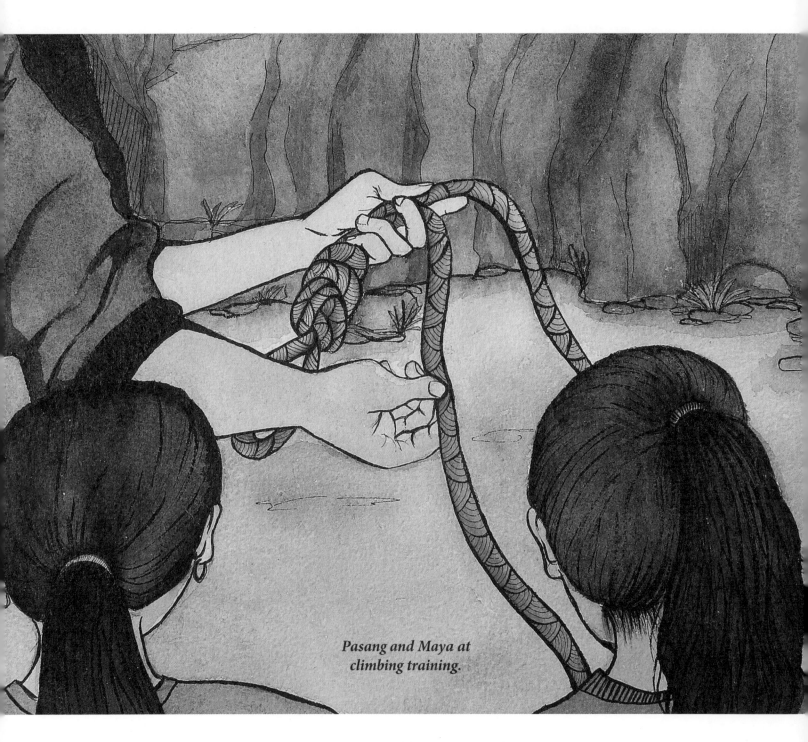

*Pasang and Maya at climbing training.*

After that, people really encouraged me to climb Everest, since Nangpai Gosum is technically even harder than Everest. In 2007, Pemba Dorje and Da Gombo asked me to join their Everest Expedition team led by Ken Noguchi of Japan. I was lucky because even though I was strong on Nangpai Gosum and people said "Everest will be easy for you", no other company would hire a woman expedition worker on an 8,000 m peak.

Just before the expedition, at training session I fell and injured my back. I needed back therapy. It was then that I met my future husband, a physiotherapist. He treated me for three hours a day for three days and the pain went away. Although I was in terrible condition at base camp, I made it to the summit of Everest. I had achieved a dream.

Maya and I met in a training session and we both decided that we wanted to climb a difficult mountain together. After thinking for a long time, we decided on K2 in 2008 but we realized that we needed more training and experience.

We decided to climb other mountains to gain experience for K2.

Travelling has always taught me so many things, such as how fortunte I am. When I am in Kathmandu or any other big city, I desire more comfort but when I am in other remote areas of Nepal, like Humla or Dolpo, I feel lucky to have been born in the Khumbu region.

In remote areas, even though people do not have much they are happy all the time. They are always smiling. They know how to live.

After facing life's challenges, I now feel I can do anything that comes my way. Even if I fall to zero, I know I am strong enough to survive. I do not feel scared.

Many people think that just because we are Sherpa, we know mountaineering from birth. There are physical and mental challenges for all women in mountaineering.

*Maya enjoyed playing sports with the boys.*

# MAYA
## Determination and Courage

I was sporty in nature from an early age, which made me different from most Nepali girls. As a teenager, I played volleyball and trained in weightlifting and boxing enough to play in the national games. I was fearless and I did not hesitate to fight with boys when they teased other girls.

There is an enormous difference in our society between girls and boys. There are so many rules saying girls should not do this or that. I always challenged those rules by doing things they said girls should not do.

Seeing my behavior, my father's friends would say to him, "We do not know about your other children, but your daughter Maya will do something when she grows up." I also thought that I would do something, and not just stay in the village. I felt bad seeing girls getting married as young as 15-16 years of age and having so many children.

I was born in 1978 in Ripal village of Okhaldhunga district, in the hills south of the Everest area. My grandfather and father had land, so people considered us rich, but every member of the family used to work equally. After school, I would do household chores to cut grass and wood even though I was not interested in doing those things.

I did not get a chance to eat what I liked, wear what I liked. I had to work when I wanted to play. These things taught me a lesson.

At the age of seven, I came to Kathmandu from my village and stayed with my uncle. I went to government school where I studied until class 10. I visited my family in Okhaldhunga just once a year during my long vacation and

*Maya would fight with the boys who were teasing girls.*

sometimes my father would come to Kathmandu during the trekking season and visit me. He sometimes worked as a trekking guide.

My family moved to Kathmandu when I was 19 and by then I had finished my intermediate schooling and was looking for a job. I roamed around searching for jobs, but I could not find one, so I helped my mother at a restaurant.

One day my father asked me to go with him on one of his treks. He had told me about trekking but was worried that because I was brought up in Kathmandu, maybe I would find it difficult. He was also worried that the high altitude might affect me. I told him right away that I would take the opportunity if there was one.

Even though I had little knowledge or experience trekking, I took the chance to guide a British female trekker through the Arun Valley for 40 days. The 40-day trek went by with me saying 'yes, no, and thank you'. After the trek, the client complained about me at the office because I really did not have any idea what I was doing and my English was so weak! The office suggested that I take some training and improve my English.

That was in 2001. I was only 23 and there were not many women trekking guides. Despite my mediocre performance, the word spread in the trekking community that I was a trekking guide.

My family began to ask around about my career. My cousin worked for a trekking business that was looking for a woman guide. They offered me a job. I took the chance and the group leader, Dan Mazur, helped me a lot so I continued guiding from that agency.

I faced many challenges as a woman trekking guide. Our own Nepali brothers would sometimes talk in a dominating way, tease, or use vulgar words. I pretended not to hear them.

One day, the Managing Director called me to his office and asked me how I felt about climbing. I had no idea about mountaineering. I was just building my skills in trekking, but still I told him that I wanted to try climbing and would take the chance if I had one. So, he sent me to Manaslu to gain experience on high passes, and to acclimatize to high altitude. In 2003 at the age of 25 I took a basic climbing course. I was the only woman participant out of 25 trainees.

Afterwards, in 2003, I went on an Ama Dablam expedition. It is a technically difficult mountain. Many of the expedition members were supportive, but some tried to discourage me.

However, I did not let down my self-esteem and continued. The climb was difficult, but I summited Ama Dablam, becoming the first Nepali woman to do so.

As a small girl, I always wanted to achieve big dreams and now, here I was on TV. For one month, my interviews were everywhere in the Nepali newspapers but, I was still not satisfied. I had to do more. I went on a second, third and fourth expedition. Every time I came back successful.

I became the first Nepali woman to climb several mountains because there were not many Nepali women climbers. Most have only climbed Everest, but not other 7,000 or 8,000 m peaks. Before climbing any mountain, I would always check to see if a Nepali woman had climbed it or not; if not then I would think I must be the first Nepali woman to climb this mountain.

At that time, most girls would marry by the age of 23. My family was starting to pressure me. My parents would often talk about this boy or that boy that I should go meet. I would tell them that I had just begun mountaineering and would like to continue with this. I knew that in our society it would be difficult to go out climbing after marriage.

Two years after I started climbing, I met my soon to be husband on an expedition. We talked and talked. I told him that I still want to climb more and shared my dreams with him. We became good friends. Then I thought it might be good to have a partner who climbs so I would get to climb more mountains. Things started becoming easy. I got even more support after I married him.

Meanwhile, Pasang and I had that dream of K2 in our mind even though both of us were busy. After having my daughter, Roos Dawa, I was confident that nothing bad would happen to me. I had faith that I would come back safely.

We have to sacrifice something in order to achieve something. My husband and I have climbed together on big mountains. Now, with our daughter, when he is on the mountain, I stay at home and vice versa.

If we really want to do something different, or to prove ourselves, we can always find a way at any age. Where there is hope, there is a way. We should not feel old in our minds. Even after marriage or children, you can do something. If you keep making up excuses, then you cannot do anything.

If you really want to change, you can.

# CHAPTER 2:
## DREAMS AND DETERMINATION, DOUBTS AND DILEMMAS

# DREAMS AND DETERMINATION

**Maya:** I could have chosen another profession, but from an early age I loved sports and adventure. When people said that as a woman, I would not be able to handle those challenges, I became angry. I would not show my anger, but kept it in my heart, worked hard, and showed them by doing. Sometimes, it is hard to find an opportunity, but it can be harder to keep and make the best of that opportunity. It needs determination.

If something happens to me, my daughter has her father and family to take care of her. This is what I think and feel. People will not sit and cry about someone for their entire life. They will mourn for couple of years and slowly things will get back to normal.

**Pasang:** There are many books on expeditions and mountaineering, but no book writes about what the climbing sherpa guides did. There is no special book that says *"the sherpa guide cooked my meal, helped me put on my shoes, tied my shoe-laces, put on my crampons, laid out the routes, and carried my oxygen cylinders. The guide supported me while risking their own life to help me reach my goal in such a freezing and unstable environment."*

These are hidden realities, the bitter truth. The 'sherpas' are the true guides on an expedition, they are not just porters.

**Maya:** Pasang and Dawa had trained and climbed many mountains together. I had never climbed with either of them before. At the time when Pasang and I started talking about climbing K2 in 2008, Dawa had not even started climbing. Later, Dawa told Pasang of her interest to climb K2. In 2013 they came to my house to talk about a K2 trip. We started to make plans.

After Dawa failed her Nepal Mountaineering Association guide exam in 2014 she was feeling sad. I went over to her house. This was how the conversation about K2 really got going.

**Dawa:** We heard so many stories about K2, that it was so dangerous to climb, a 'killer' mountain. I wanted to see for myself whether K2 really was the hardest mountain.

I became determined to climb K2. It was my dream to climb an 8,000 m mountain and K2 was my biggest dream. K2 is so risky that all climbers fear it. It was a different expedition because we

had never climbed together. We were excited, and all shared the same goal – to climb K2.

Even if we failed, we thought it would be a good thing to try.

# DOUBTS AND DILEMMAS

**Pasang :** The big icefall avalanche happened on Everest in 2014[1], just three months before we were going to climb K2. I was there and saw the avalanche kill or injure so many friends. At first, I felt we should not go to K2 .

On Everest, if you break your leg, you can manage to go down; on K2, there are no good places for support and rest. I read somewhere 'K2 - No way down' and wondered what that meant. Later I discovered that it means, 'climb carefully and get down - or die.' The route is so narrow that it is impossible to rescue someone.

In Nepal, we have 'long line rescue' and can pay 5,000 dollars to call a helicopter. In Pakistan there is no good rescue system on K2. Helicopters are controlled by the army and the cost of calling a helicopter from Islamabad is 30,000 dollars.

My husband, asked me, "Being a human should we not keep the other human happy?

"Yes, we have to," I replied.

Then he said, "Why are you making everyone upset? Why are you torturing everyone? We cannot sleep at night thinking about you and your plan."

His words touched my heart. He does not have real life experience climbing mountains; his experience of them is only through the books he reads. That scares him. I know how it is on the mountains so told him that it is more dangerous to drive in Kathmandu than to climb mountains.

---

1 In April 2014, 16 expedition workers died in the Khumbu Icefall while climbing from base camp to Camp 1 on Everest. A serac (huge block of glacial ice) broke off from a hanging glacier above and swept down.

**Dawa:** Pasang was very upset when she returned to Kathmandu after the big avalanche on Everest. She would not pick up our calls because she had seen the disaster with her own eyes. Pasang told everyone at base camp that from this moment on, she would never climb a mountain again.

Maya and I went to her house and waited quietly in the living room for her. When she came from her room, she was surprised to see us. We talked to her about continuing K2 plans.

After a week, she was excited again, had good energy, and worked hard to raise funds. I wanted Pasang to go because I had climbed with her many times and felt comfortable with her in the mountains. I had never climbed with Maya before.

**Maya:** I felt terrible about the big disaster on Everest. Sixteen Sherpas had died. We did not say a word about K2 for a week. It was a hard time for everyone. I went to visit the victims in hospital and to help the families of the deceased doing funeral rituals.

Weeks passed with condolence events for the deceased. We attended all the meetings conducted by Nepal Mountaineering Association. Many young Sherpas had died leaving wives and children behind. Their children were too young to understand what was going on. I saw their wives with eyes full of tears. I felt so bad.

I thought of my own daughter, Rooz. If I die, what would she do, what would her life be like?

I realized that my personal dreams, name, and fame are not everything. As a mother, I need to take care of my daughter and family. I was in a dilemma as it was too late to postpone the expedition. By then we had received money from many sources and our expedition was all over the media and news.

My husband would say, "It is not very dangerous but you have to be careful. You have experience and you have good technical skills. Everything will be fine. Accidents occur on every mountain, big or small. Take care of yourself and be careful." Although he was always supportive, my parents were still worried. They cried when I was leaving for K2. When I had left for other expeditions, no one cried. Now that I was leaving for K2, everybody cried.

# PLANS AND MORE DOUBTS

**Maya:** We had only four months to prepare to climb K2 so we worked around the clock. At night, I would see my daughter and husband sleeping peacefully beside me while many things played in my mind until I turned off the laptop to sleep.

Everest is the highest mountain of all, however in the world of mountaineering you gain more recognition if you have successfully summitted K2. Even if you climb Everest ten times, people respect you more if you climb K2 just once.

I lost two kilos running around to prepare documents for our expedition. During those weeks of planning and preparation for K2, I sacrificed my time with my family and my daughter.

We collected funds until the very last day before our flight to Pakistan. It was a rush until the last hour. We caught our breath only after our plane left from Kathmandu Airport.

We were finally going to K2 and that was a very comfortable feeling after overcoming all sorts of pressure from family, funding and everything

for the expedition. Besides, I had learned so many things during this phase, including that we probably needed more training and experience for K2.

**Dawa:** Maya worked hardest on the paperwork for the K2 expedition because Pasang and I were busy climbing other mountains at that time. Maya handled the finances. As a senior climbing leader, we viewed Maya as the boss.

I thought that this was my one and only chance to go to K2. It would not be good to go back repeatedly like on Everest. When we were leaving from Kathmandu, we never expected to come back together. I wondered if something would happen to one of us or if one of us might even die. I never expected that we would come back safe and successfully together.

It was a tough time and our families were worried about us. My family was upset with my decision. Although they did not express their sadness, I saw that they were not happy. They told me that I should do an easy job or settle abroad, but I was determined.

The closer we were to actually leaving for K2, the more we tried to talk to every person we knew thinking that it might be our last chance to see them. We were happy to be leaving for K2 but on the other side, it was hard to leave everyone behind. On the day of our flight, people came to wish us a successful journey. It was a difficult moment at Kathmandu airport where everyone was crying and hugging each other.

In mountaineering, when you leave your home you never know whether you will come back or not. We had been on many expeditions, but our families had never bid farewell to us by offering katas (ceremonial scarves). In our culture, people usually do not offer a kata to someone going on an expedition but for K2 our necks were loaded with katas. My heart was beating faster than before, I thought it might be the final goodbye.

# CHAPTER 3:
# JOURNEY TO THE MOUNTAIN:
# PAKISTAN

# GOING TO PAKISTAN

**Dawa:** At Kathmandu airport, we changed our clothes and wore conventional Pakistani salwar kurta (scarf, baggy pants, and long smock). We could not find the right size in ready-made kurtas, so we had ours sewn quickly. It was summer, so it was cooler to wear a kurta than jeans.

Luckily, three Sherpa men who were also going to climb K2 were at the airport - Mingma Gyalzen, Densa Bhote, and Zamling Bhote. Densa was funny, always cracked jokes, and helped us escape the boring wait at the airport. We were anxious to be on our way.

It took us four hours to get to Islamabad. The three Sherpa men were staying at the same hotel. Pakistani friends met us at the airport and dropped us at the hotel.

**Maya:** The city was neat, clean, and uncrowded. The roads were good. The security system was good. There were army camps even in isolated places and they checked everyone thoroughly.

In our Sherpa community woman are independent. They go out, work, and have control of the house. Sherpa women are hard workers who can earn a living on their own. In the villages, Sherpa women do every task. Those without an education tend to their yaks and zopkyok to transport trekking and expedition goods. In Pakistan, we did not see any women on the roads or anywhere. In Nepal, women walk everywhere freely. We were keen to see some women. It was so different from what I was used to seeing. Although we did not see any women, we did see many young girls going to school wearing long kurtas and veils covering their faces.

**Pasang:** There was a big welcome for us on our arrival from Pakistan's senior climbers Nazir Sabhir, the first Pakistani to stand on top of Everest and former president of the Tourism Board of Pakistan, and Ashraf Aman, the first Pakistani to summit K2.

They often said, 'Inshallah sab thik ho jayega', which means 'if God wills, everything will be all right'. That sounded so beautiful. Everybody had warned us that K2 is so difficult and dangerous that we might die there. So we enjoyed every moment as if it was our last. We danced until 1am at night and slept until seven in the morning. We were trying not to worry at all.

It is mandatory for Pakistani women to cover their heads with a veil or scarf in public. There is no problem if Western women tourists do not cover their heads, but as Asian women, we dressed in formal Pakistani clothes and covered our heads in respect for their culture. We became like Pakistani women for the time.

# ON THE ROAD TO THE MOUNTAIN

**Dawa:** It was difficult as a woman climber in Pakistan. There were many men who would stare as if they had never seen women before. The climbers and our porters were very nice but most people in Skardu were so curious. Going out to the toilet alone was scary, so we had to go with someone. In Nepal, we go alone to the toilet but here we could not even hike alone. We always stayed together.

Since we looked different from Pakistani girls, men came to take photos with us. They behaved as if we were celebrities. If they were respectful, we allowed a picture with them but if they behaved strangely, we walked away. We felt safe because we were travelling with the Sherpa men from Nepal. Without them, we would not have felt comfortable.

We heard that the road north to the Karakorum was dangerous, so we decided to try to fly to Skardu. Unfortunately, our flight did not take off due to bad weather. The weather showed no signs of improvement after two days so on the second afternoon we decided to travel by road.

We had a great trip for the first 4-5 hours looking at the beautiful landscape. On our way, we saw an old woman working in the field. As soon as she saw men in the group, she hid behind a rock. We only saw small children because girls older than 14 years do not come outside.

We had planned to stop for the night at Chilas but we heard it was not safe so we kept going. It took us 16 hours to reach Skardu with 12 people in a big jeep and two drivers taking turns.

In Skardu, the other climbers asked us to leave for base camp straight away, but since we were so tired after two long days of driving, we stayed there overnight.

*Since we were women, our Pakistani driver took us to his home to meet his family.*

The next morning, the three of us took a jeep and left for Askole. Although the road was dangerous, our driver was good. His house was on the way. He took us inside and introduced us to his wife and eight daughters. Usually the men here do not introduce their wives or women relatives to outsiders but since we were all women, he allowed them to meet us.

His wife offered us salted butter tea and biscuits, which reminded us of our Tibetan tea in our homes. The cups they used were the same as we Sherpas use in our homes. The culture was similar. We left 500 rupees to thank her.

The jeep ride ended at Askole. We started walking at seven the next morning. It was one of the hardest days. The weather was so hot that we developed blisters and the wind damaged my umbrella. There was no food or water. We were thirsty and very tired.

# WALKING ON POINTY ROCKS

**Dawa:** Sharp pointed rocks covered the glacier and trail, so we had to walk on rocks all the way. After trekking for many days, we reached Broad Peak base camp and went to K2 base camp after lunch the following day. We took the wrong way on the glacier but luckily, a Pakistani man saw us and directed us on the right path. Many people were helpful and had a good sense of humour.

The trek to Everest through Khumbu is so beautiful, but the journey to K2 base camp was the most difficult trek that I have ever done. Just pointy rocks everywhere!

When we arrived at K2 base camp, everyone came out of their tents to welcome us. When we were working as 'sherpas' in previous expeditions, we had to set up everything ourselves. As clients on K2, we did not have to do this work.

**Maya:** I was back to the mountains after five years. I had put on weight after having a child and I was not used to the 45 degree heat on the glacier. So I was always thirsty and got blisters on my feet. I got tired quickly and went slowly.

Most of the climbing team had already reached Camp 1 and Camp 2 when we arrived at base camp. The weather was bad so we stayed in base camp for a week. Here, a Pakistani asked us if we had any "masala". In Nepali masala means spices used in cooking, so our cook told him we had lots of masala and showed him all the spices in our kitchen. Only then did I learn that in Urdu 'Masala' means 'problem'!

We decided to start our climb after we performed the rituals to honour the mountain deities and prayed for a successful expedition as we do in Sherpa culture. We do not climb unless we perform these prayers at the base camp. We did our Sherpa rituals on Monday, as we believed it to be an auspicious day for all three of us.

*Pointy rocks covered the trail and glacier.*

# CHAPTER 4:
# CLIMBING THE 'SAVAGE' MOUNTAIN

*We spent eight days in basecamp with the bad weather.*

# BASECAMP

**Pasang:** It snowed while we were at base camp, so we had to stay there for eight days. To kill time, we visited the camps of other teams and talked to them. Oddly enough, we also danced.

The people in this area of Pakistan believe that dancing in the base camp pleases the mountain goddess who in return ensures clear weather. Although Pakistani women do not dance with men, the Pakistanis were thrilled when we danced with them.

We did not know if we would succeed in reaching the summit, but Dawa dreamed of a woman dressed in white sitting on her pillow. When she told us about the dream, Maya said that it was a good sign of success and that she had dreamnt of a white-haired woman in a white dress the first time she climbed Ama Dablam. It was a successful expedition, so she believed the dream was a good omen.

Since we arrived late, the other climbers had already set up Camps 1 and 2 and returned to base camp. Ropes had been set up to climb up to Camp 3, but we did not know if ropes could be set all the way up the last ridge to the summit. We held a meeting at base camp with the other expedition teams about setting a fixed rope up the highest section of the mountain. We collected some ropes from the other teams that the Pakistani staff members would carry up the mountain for the sherpa guides to fix in place.

We were worried that if the weather turned bad coming back down the mountain, we could lose our way. Indeed, many accidents on K2 have happened when people could not find their way down on the descent. We thought that we should put in an extra rope to go from the end of the fixed rope at the top of the Bottleneck to the summit to guide us down the correct route.

Our team had hired professional climbers, who were the same Sherpa ethnic group as us, to work as sherpa guides and manage the expedition. Each of us had one sherpa guide to climb with us in case we had problems.

*We climbed slowly up the steep snow and rock slope.*

# CLIMBING, CLIMBING, CLIMBING

**Maya:** There were four camps to stay in on the way up the mountain and we left early in the morning to reach Camp 1. We climbed slowly up the steep snow and rock slope. With each step we struggled to breathe.

Sometimes, our crampons scratched on rocks in the snow. Still, we managed to reach Camp 1 early in the day. Pasang and Dawa decided to push on to try to reach Camp 2 but just 30 minutes below it, Pasang had problems with her ankle. Since our two guides, Pemba and Nima, were carrying two tents, we decided to set up camp here at this cold, windy spot. It was just below one of the most difficult parts of the climb, the House Chimney.

All night long, we could hear avalanches on the nearby peaks and worried that an avalanche might come down on us. It was our first night on the mountain and we were too scared to sleep.

The next morning, we hoped to get to Camp 2, but the wind was so strong that we had to turn back. A day later, we again started climbing up to Camp 2 when eight of us stopped below the House Chimney, a huge crack in the cliff over 100 feet tall.

Every other possible route had too many avalanches. Everyone said that this was the safest way to climb higher on K2 even though the crack was just a bit wider than our shoulders and climbing up it is really difficult. It was rock climbing at high altitude[2] and so hard to breathe.

The first steps were tricky on thin ice coating the sloping rocks. We looked up at the rock walls towering above us. We used our jumars on the fixed rope, sometimes putting our feet on small ledges or an old ladder that the wind blew back and forth in the chimney.

The tricky part was having to brace ourselves with our legs across the chimney while we took our jumars off the rope to move them above the anchors. We just kept on climbing up to the top of the chimney.

There was another steep slope to reach Camp 2, which was nothing more than a sloping spot

[2] http://www.alanarnette.com/blog/2014/07/19/k2-housess-chimney-camp-2/

*The climbing route was constantly steep up.*

carved out of the snow. The area was just big enough for the 16 tents of all the expeditions. Although it was less vertical than the slope it was still steep enough that we had to watch every step and be roped the whole time we were in Camp 2. If we slipped, there was nothing to stop our fall.

The route was constantly steep up, up, and up! There were no flat sections like there are on Everest or some other mountains. When the sun went down at 4pm, it was freezing cold. We bundled up in our tent to rest and wait for the morning.

48

**Dawa:** *"Maya had her own sleeping bag, so she slept well. Pasang and I were sharing one sleeping bag, so we were freezing. I did not sleep well because of the cold."*

After a long cold night, we set off in the morning for Camp 3. We made our way up the slippery ice-coated rocks of the Black Pyramid. Snow and ice covered its almost-vertical cliffs. As we were clambering up, stones started rolling down. Some stones hit Maya's leg making a big blue bruise. The three of us stayed together until we finished climbing this rocky ridge. From there, we each went at our own pace.

Our guides trudged ahead of us carrying the tents and supplies. We helped them to set up Camp 3 but it was hard to break the ice to make good platforms where we could pitch the tents. We were above the Black Pyramid, but right below some steep snow slopes that often avalanched.

The weather was good the next day as we started climbing the steep snow slopes up to Camp 4 at 8,000 m. When we reached, clouds blew in wrapping us in mist and blowing snow. We couldn't even see the next tent. It was a complete 'white out'. We crawled inside our tent for the rest of the afternoon and night.

We had brought tsampa (roasted barley) and chilli to make our meal. First, we served the sherpa guide team fixing the ropes and then the other climbing members. Everyone enjoyed the meal before trying to sleep for the night.

## GOING FOR THE PEAK

On July 25, we left Camp 4 at 11pm. It was the start of a long night and day to reach the summit and come down as quickly as possible. It can be extremely hard to get back down. We only had 600 m in elevation to climb but had to face the challenges of climbing in the dark, the high altitude, extremely cold temperatures, fierce winds and rock hard snow and ice. Plus, we faced the extreme risks of falling ice from the hanging glacier. It was safer to start in the night at the coldest time, because there was less risk of avalanches.

*The great risk was ice falling from the hanging glacier.*

The Bottleneck is the most dangerous part of the route up K2. If the overhanging ice breaks and huge chunks of ice fall, they can hit the climbers or cut their ropes, leaving them with no rope for safety and support while descending.

The Bottleneck was two parts. First we had to climb straight up the Bottleneck's narrow couloir of ice and snow. Then, just when we thought we had finished the Bottleneck we had to traverse along the bottom of a huge wall of vertical ice. We felt so tiny below this ice cliff.

The sherpa guides were still fixing ropes across this traverse part of the Bottleneck so we had to wait. We stood stuck in the middle of the Bottleneck for about three hours. Our feet were cold because it took such a long time. Here we were in a big traffic jam of climbers standing on a ledge on a vertical icy cliff. Even climbers who had started very late from Camp 4 caught up and were waiting here.

Our base camp kept calling us wondering where we were. They were surprised to hear us keep saying "Bottleneck" every time. It was 3am when we started across the Bottleneck. It was too dangerous for us to traverse it together, so we had to move one by one. This took more time.

Finally, our team all crossed the Bottleneck and reached the end of the fixed ropes. We wondered what would happen if the clouds came in on our way down from the summit; there weren't any ropes to show us the way back to this spot.

We gathered extra thin ropes to put on the route to and from the summit to show us the way back down to the fixed ropes at the Bottleneck.

Everyone had an extra rope in their packs, so added their rope to the line.

Gradually, we had enough ropes to reach the 200 m to the summit. The ropes were all tangled so Dawa was untangling them while Pasang tied the ropes together as the sherpa guides led the way up the ridge.

The four sherpa guides on our team carried the ropes and broke the trail. If we had enough rope, we would reach the summit in 4-5 hours and come down in 10-12 hours.

The summit was not far but it was so difficult because the snow was sugary and wouldn't stick together or to the ice beneath it. If we slipped and fell, it would be impossible to use the ice axe to stop ourselves sliding in such snow. We kept slogging up through this slippery snow. The uphill seemed like it would never end.

Then suddenly, at 3:35pm on July 26, we emerged onto a large open slope.

The summit, finally!

We had climbed up to 8,611 m, but more importantly, we had climbed the 'killer' savage mountain.

Everyone from the teams crowded onto this area. We all took turns taking photographs.

**Maya:** *"I was crying inside as I got to the summit. I could not cry tears, or they would freeze on my face and oxygen mask."*

We had been climbing for over 16 hours and could see clouds coming so we didn't stay long on the summit. The clouds covered the summit once we were about 50 m below it on the way down.

**Dawa:** *"When I reached the top of K2, my oxygen was almost empty. I took pictures with Maya and Pasang and turned around to go quickly. I did not tell Maya and Pasang that I was leaving. I had my supporting sherpa guide and he was there at the top taking lots of pictures. He had five cameras in his hands. I told him that we must go down quickly."*

*Maya, Dawa and Pasang on the summit of K2 on July 26, 2014.*

# CHAPTER 5:
# HOMEWARD BOUND: BUT FIRST,
# A TREACHEROUS DESCENT

# THE TREACHEROUS DESCENT

**Dawa:** Suddenly, it was so cloudy that I couldn't see anything on the way back down. I had no clue where I was, or where Pasang and Maya were. When I thought of them, I stopped and waited for five minutes.

Then I started to worry because I had so little oxygen left, I thought that if I could manage to get to the Bottleneck, I could manage without oxygen after that. I scrambled down as fast as I could. Then my sherpa guide came along so we descended together.

We followed the thin extra rope line that our team had set down to the Bottleneck where the 'official' fixed lines started. The rope was just to guide us down to the Bottleneck.

**Pasang:** The extra rope line we had set from the Bottleneck to the summit made the whole expedition successful. Without it, descending in a whiteout would have been impossible.

At first, it didn't seem necessary to put the extra rope line because the trail looked easy but we knew that this section was where many people had made mistakes and accidents had happened. The whiteout on K2 was so serious

we could not even see our own feet! The wind had covered all our old footprints with snow. The drop off is steep on both sides; one mistake and you are gone.

We warned everyone not to use the extra rope line to hold their weight because the anchors were not strong enough to hold many climbers. We had used an ice axe to anchor it because there was no proper ice screw or snow bar. Above that, there was another anchor made of an old oxygen cylinder. These would have been safe anchors for good snow, but the snow was too soft and sugary for them to be safe if they had too much weight on them.

The ice axe anchor held because the sherpa guides had buried it properly. In fact, the extremely cold temperature froze the ice axe to the ice. We were lucky in every aspect. The weather was not good, the anchor was not that strong, but nothing bad happened. In the end, everyone appreciated the rope line on the descent.

**Dawa:** As I was crossing the Bottleneck, the wind blew snow all over my face and back. Right then, I thought that some ice above the

*Dawa descending quickly after her oxygen ran out.*

Bottleneck had collapsed. That was my scariest moment on K2 as I could not see the rope. I finally reached Camp 4 in the dark at 8pm. It had taken me 21 hours to reach the summit and come down.

I crashed out totally exhausted into our tent. At about 10pm, I woke up. Pasang was with me but I wondered about Maya. Pasang and I could not talk, we just stared at each other wondering about Maya. Finally, I woke up again an hour later and there was the blue down suit in the tent. Maya was back with us.

**Maya:** In the whiteout on the way down, we could not see the route clearly so my sherpa guide and I were scrambling down together above the Bottleneck. It was windy and snowing. I really could not see so I traded my goggles with him but it didn't help, so I just kept slogging down.

At one point I fell. I could see that someone else had fallen at the same spot. I had jumped thinking that I would manage with the rope, but I fell with the snow.

The snow was so soft that the more I tried to get up the more I fell. Finally, I called my sherpa guide to help me. Later, when I told Dawa and Pasang that I fell in the same spot where

someone else had fallen ahead of me Pasang smiled and said that it was her.

When I recall those moments, I sometimes wonder if I should have done things another way. Now I cannot go back to the past.

**Dawa:** The next morning, my oxygen had ran out so my face was swollen. My guide found some oxygen for me, then the swelling went down. We packed up Camp 4 and started to head down. Descending was not that easy. Rocks kept falling as other climbers descended through the rocky areas.

Maya decided to stay in Camp 2 that night, but Pasang and I went down to Advance Base Camp. It was dark by the time we reached there at 9pm. Our sherpa guides were there to help us.

**Maya:** Even after we crossed the Bottleneck, we were still worried. The way down was just as dangerous with falling rocks and ice. We had not yet called anyone to say we had made it to the summit. If we had shared the news from Camp 4, then they would have started celebrating our achievement. What if we didn't make it all the way back to base camp? So, we didn't call anyone and waited until we were all back at base camp before calling home.

*Maya fell in the soft snow... but so had Pasang.*

Route: Abruzzi Ridge

**Elevations**
Summit: 28,251'/ 8611m
Camp 4: 25,080'/ 7600 m
Camp 3: 23,760'/ 7200 m
Camp 2: 22,110'/ 6700 m
Camp 1: 19,965'/ 6050 m
Base Camp: 18,650'/ 5650 m

# HOMEWARD BOUND

**Dawa:** I felt it was a miracle when we all reached base camp. I still couldn't believe that we had all made the summit and come back safely.

We stayed in base camp for one day to pack our tents and belongings. We were in a hurry to get home so we decided to walk two camps in a day from base camp. We did not have enough food and water, walking in the heat and sun. The second day was the hardest of all. We started walking at 5am to reach our destination at 4pm. Our support group arrived at nine in the evening.

**Maya:** Although I have done a lot of climbing, this expedition was very different from the point of view of my family and loved ones. I had more fun than difficulties, but my family was worried day and night. When the time came for us to go home, I cried thinking about my daughter. I wanted to hear her voice, but I knew I would cry if I did.

Finally, at Kathmandu airport, my eyes were full of tears when I saw her. She was right there waiting for me. We had overcome so many obstacles in our quest to climb K2.

# ONWARDS

**Pasang:** We were lucky, we made it to the summit on our first attempt; some groups fail to reach the summit even after four or five attempts. We are the first South Asian women to be on top of K2. Many men in our climbing community assumed that they would easily climb K2 after our successful summit. However, no one made it to the summit for three years after our expedition.

We had calls from the press asking for our summit photos, but they did not ask for the story. If they were serious journalists, they would have been keen to know the stories rather than simply have a summit photo. Our story is more important than the photos. We decided not to provide our summit photo to anyone, as we wanted to do our own press conference and only then provide the photos.

**Dawa:** I wanted good pictures for proof in case some people tried to dispute our achievement. National Geographic wanted to write a story, so we gave them the summit photos. They wrote a good story, but their title "Controversial Women's Expedition", was confusing. By controversial, they meant it was not a women-only expedition. This made some people in Nepal think that we did not make it to the summit because they just read the title, not whole the story.

**Maya:** We are very happy that we met our goal. No one expected the three of us to summit and come back safely. When we started, no one directly tried to stop us, but most people warned us. Everyone was surprised in the end.

Now I would like to fulfill my responsibility towards my community with all my ability and thank everyone for their kind support and contributions to our success.

Our journey should send a message to young people, especially girls that to achieve something in life one must constantly try. One must never give up. There will be many objections and obstacles, but you must keep doing what you like doing. Most Nepali parents think that once their daughters reach a certain age, they must get married. That is not the only important thing in our lives. Women must set examples in various fields. Then people will hear and follow us.

Now, we must use our experiences to work to help our own country. It is important for us to share our ideas with young people and new climbers. Everyone will encounter positive and negative feedback. We must be positive while considering the negative, but not let it hold us back.

I am proud of what our whole team accomplished. It is a great achievement and the world now knows that there are strong women in Nepal.

# THE CLIMB GOES ON...

Each member of the team has accomplishments in the years since their success on K2.

The team came back together to climb Kanchenjunga in 2017 but could not reach the summit with the long route above 8,000 m.

## Maya:

In 2016, I climbed Manaslu, Everest for the third time, and Himlung. Since then, I am working for my own company. Our team had a plan to climb again. Since we had all climbed Everest and K2, we wanted to do Kanchenjunga as 'three women and three summits', and attempt the world's third highest peak. We failed to reach the summit in 2017. Then in 2018, Dawa was busy and Pasang was pregnant, so I went with another team and got to within 80 m of the summit but had to turn around due to the conditions. Finally, in 2019, I summited Kanchenjunga.

Dawa and I climbed together again in Russia on Mount Elbrus. Then, I went with women from many countries to Kenya. This was a great experience. Now I am focussing on climbing all 14 of the 8,000 m peaks. I will try to find some sponsors. I am active on the boards of Nepal Mountaineering Association and Everest Summiteers Association. I keep busy guiding climbs and treks, giving motivational speeches, promoting tourism in Nepal, and spending time with my daughter.

## Dawa:

I became the first Nepali woman to climb Makalu and the first Asian woman to pass the International Federation of Mountain Guides Associations (IFMGA) certification. I am one of ten women in the world with this certification so I can guide all over the world – in Russia, South America, and the US, especially in Alaska. I guided the 2019 National Geographic Scientific Expedition to install a weather station on Everest. I focus on guiding and teaching. For my own climbing, I like to do smaller, technical peaks making first ascents.

I am now a global athlete with North Face and am the first Nepali to represent an international company. This changes the perception of climbers from being workers to being athletes who work internationally. I hope this inspires the younger generation, especially as women.

I help with the 'Stop Girl Trafficking' program of the American Himalayan Foundation by providing outdoor education to young women at Khumbu Climbing Centre. For nine months a year, I am busy guiding. Then for some of the time, I like to give back by teaching girls and volunteering with the Nomad Clinic's medical camps in remote districts such as Dolpo and Humla. I like to have a balance between volunteering, being a global athlete, and guiding. My big dream is to try Everest without oxygen.

## Pasang:

Within a year of our climb, the big earthquake happened in Nepal. I worked very hard with my husband and friends to help people in remote villages. Later that year, I was nominated for the National Geographic Adventurer of the Year. People from all over the world voted. To my surprise, I won this award in 2016.

I've also gone on several Nomad Clinic treks to help with translation between the doctors and nurses and the people in these remote districts. It was on one of these treks when I realised that I was pregnant.

My son was born a few months later. He is the joy of my life. Now, I am busy with my family. In the fall of 2019, I guided a climbing trip for the first time since I gave birth. My son came along. He loves the mountains – just like his mama.

# GLOSSARY

**ALTITUDE ACCLIMATIZATION** - the process of adjusting to lessening oxygen levels at higher elevations, in order to avoid altitude sickness.

**ANCHOR** - Any solid, fixed point of attachment with which climbers connect themselves usually via rope, to a cliff or slope to prevent a fall, lift a load, or redirect a rope.

**AVALANCHE** - a tumbling mass of snow and/or ice that slides down a mountain slope.

**CHIMNEY** - a crack wide enough for a climber's body to fit inside. The climber often uses his or her head, back and feet to apply opposite pressure on the vertical walls.

**COULOIR** - steep, narrow, passages through cliff bands.

**CRAMPONS** - metal framework with spikes that attaches to boots to walk on glaciers or climb ice.

**FIXED ROPE** - rope fixed at an anchor or attachment point.

**GLACIER** - Year-round ice covering a large area. Formed by many years of snow accumulating and eventually solidifying into ice. Glaciers are often expanding or shrinking. They have many features, such as seracs, which add to the challenges of safe travel.

**JUMAR** - A type of mechanical ascender to climb up on a rope.

**MOUNTAINEERING** - climbing mountains using special equipment and techniques for rock, ice, or snow.

**ROPE** - Long ropes specifically for climbing, of varying diameter and material, dynamic or static.

**ROUTE** - certain path to climb a rock or mountain.

**SERAC** - block or tower of ice on a steep glacier. Seracs form as glaciers creep over vertical cliffs—cracking the ice.

**SHERPA** - a person of the ethnic group of the name Sherpa, that originated in the Himalaya. Also, a generic term for mountaineering guides and expedition workers in Nepal (usually those working at or above base camp) regardless of their ethnic group.

**TRAVERSE** - moving horizontally across a slope or cliff.

**WHITE-OUT** - Blizzard or cloud conditions so thick that it can be impossible to determine which way is up or down, or even if one is moving or still.

# ACKNOWLEDGEMENTS

We would like to thank with all our hearts the many people and organisations who personally and financially supported our climb of K2. First our family and friends in the Sherpa and climbing communities. We received financial support from Nepal Mountaineering Association, Everest Summiteers Association, Nepal National Mountain Guide Association, Nepal Mountaineering Instructors Association, ICIMOD, private companies, and the Government of Nepal.

We thank Seven Summits Treks and Expeditions for organizing and supporting the expedition and especially Mingdorchi Sherpa and Pemba Sherpa of Tashigaon, and Nima Dorchi Sherpa of Halung, Sankhuwasabha District for supporting us on the climb. We would also like to thank Frances and her team at Mera Publications for their time and patience making this book.

**Maya Sherpa, Pasang Lhamu Sherpa Akita, and Dawa Yangzum Sherpa**

This book has been an adventure in itself. I would first like to thank the team of Maya, Dawa, and Pasang for telling me their stories.

My staff at Mera Publications have contributed in so many ways. I'd like to acknowledge Sareena Rai, Alina Chhantel, Neetu Ranjit Karmacharya, Dalima Rawal, the late Sonam Tashi Sherpa, and Tsering Zangmu Sherpa. Alina deserves special mention for her commitment and multiple drafts of the illustrations. I would also like to thank Michael Gill for editorial support. As always, Anil Shrestha's team at DigiScan have been helpful and supportive in the layout and printing of the book. To quote Anil, "We'll make it happen!"

Thanks also to Pasang Yangjee, Al, and Jenni and Conrad for their sweet words in the forewords. To quote Al, "Don't leave your dreams on your pillow."

**Frances Klatzel**
Kathmandu
February 18, 2020